The Purpose of The Kingdom Woman

How The Kingdom of God Flows

LaSonya Richardson

THE PURPOSE OF THE KINGDOM WOMAN
HOW THE KINGDOM OF GOD FLOWS

LASONYA RICHARDSON
larichh@yahoo.com

ISBN: 978-1-943342-55-6

Printed in the USA.
All rights reserved

Cover Design: JEREMIAH DEAN

Published by: Destined To Publish | Flossmoor, Illinois
www.DestinedToPublish.com

This book is dedicated to my late husband, Marcellus, who began this journey with me but had to make an early trip to Heaven to make sure my mansion would be ready when I arrived.

First, I acknowledge my sons and daughters, who listened to me as I repeated these concepts out loud, asking if they understood the point that I was trying to get across. Second, I would like to acknowledge the many women who shared their concerns about the issues they have had with work, romantic relationships, and being parents.

Table of Contents

INTRODUCTION

This book is for women who have wanted someone to come alongside them and answer the questions that have been on their minds for long. No matter what our ages, ethnicities, marital statuses, or faiths, we all have one thing in common: the pursuit of our purpose. We all desire to live lives that say that we, women, matter; that when we were born, the very world around us changed for the better; and that when we leave this earth, we will leave marks on it that are so grand that we will be remembered for generations to come.

What exactly is purpose? Purpose is that thing that enables us to understand why we were brought into this world. Purpose is the reason we get up every morning and have something to look forward to. Purpose gives us the energy and drive to pursue something until it is finished. It fills us with resolve and makes us push past every obstacle in our way. When we have purpose in our lives, it motivates us to stand, even in the face of adversity. Purpose fills our minds, and if we try to forget about it or procrastinate, the thought continues to pop up in our minds repeatedly. Purpose is the driving force that helps us achieve our goals, but if we don't achieve them, it causes us to feel frustrated.

Look at all the books that have been written on the subject. Even magazine articles claim to know the answers to finding your true purpose. It would seem that we should have all the answers we need by now. As Kingdom women in particular, we are constantly searching for our purpose as working women, wives, and womb bearers. Even though we love what we do as wives and mothers, we have realized that there must be something outside our everyday lives that we were put on Earth to do. After all, children grow up to be self-sufficient and our husbands have already been raised by their mothers.

As Kingdom women, we can no longer dwell in a place of uncertainty concerning who we were born to be and our value to the world. When God created man, woman was just as much a part of His plan. We cannot continue to see man's purpose clearly while ours seems foggy. We must not see ourselves from the perspective of those outside the Kingdom either. Neither can we view ourselves through the eyes of religion. We must be willing to dispel every lie that we were fed about our purpose and why we were created. Usually, the truth is right in front of our faces, yet because it has not been clearly explained, we cannot see it for what it is. Only when we humble ourselves can we be reintroduced to God's mind concerning us.

Because our God was very purposeful when He created us, we must be purposeful to rediscover His original purpose for us. When we discover His original purpose in creating us, we can begin to see what He wants to reflect through us on Earth. But if we don't know what that is, how can we be His reflection? And how can others see His reflection through us if we don't properly reflect His Image? Others can only develop knowledge based on what they have seen.

When God created Kingdom women, He put within them everything they would need to fulfill the purpose that He had given them. He filled Kingdom women with an array of gifts, talents, and abilities. However, these gifts, talents, and abilities do not by themselves constitute Kingdom purpose. He also gave women a hierarchy in which to operate. An example of hierarchy is the family. Here, the husband/father is the head. Then the wife/mother is next in the chain of command, and then come the children. A hierarchy organizes everyone into positions, not to restrict them, but to ensure that the Kingdom of God flows smoothly. Our purpose lies not just in what we do but also in expressing it through our God-given channels.

Furthermore, this book has a purpose, which is to give the Kingdom woman an understanding of how the Kingdom of God flows together. Our lack of understanding regarding how things flow together causes us to make mistakes that result in tremendous setbacks. We have become familiar with our professions, callings, and various gifts. But it occurs to me that although we are coming into knowledge regarding what we can do more than we have at any other time in history, we lack the understanding of how to be in step with one another. We have not yet realized that we, our gifts, and our callings are not just some free-floating planets outside any solar system or universe. Everything was made with everything else in mind. So to operate in our purpose as women in the Kingdom of God is to operate with everyone and everything else in mind. We cannot operate on solo missions without understanding how everyone else fits in.

It is imperative to go back to the beginning of recorded time and reexamine what we thought we knew about ourselves. Thus, we can cast off the old mindset that keeps us from moving beyond the preset boundaries that were placed in our paths because of others' misunderstanding. We must also learn to tear down all the preconceived boundaries that we've imposed on ourselves. We are just as guilty as everyone else when it comes to blocking who we are and what we are meant to be. So we are still looking for someone else to tell us what to do.

Although this book is addressed to women, I highly recommend that it goes through men's hands. Men have women in their lives and out in the world that they need to understand. Many of these women will find their places at the forefront. So this book should give the men a clearer view of those who will labor alongside them so that they will be ready to fulfill their God-given assignments together. Both men and women must know each other's assignments so that they can assist each other.

The Kingdom of God

What is the Kingdom of God? Some may believe it is a mystical place that exists in the movies. Maybe you think of the Kingdom of God as being derived from a fairy tale. Other people believe that the Kingdom of God only exists in a place where God is said to dwell, a place called Heaven, which is in another dimension of time and space. But the Kingdom of God is so much more expansive than that. You see, Heaven did not exist before Him. Heaven is a place that He created, and He chose it to be the place of His throne. From this place, He expresses His rule, reign, and dominion as King. You could even say that Heaven is His headquarters, which He designated. And yes, although you can't see Heaven with the naked eye, it is a very real place.

The Kingdom of God in relation to Heaven is like a woman who buys a house. The house that she buys is not yet a home. When she comes in, bringing her unique expression of the love and joy in her heart and adorning the atmosphere, it becomes a home. Since a house is just a physical thing, she could choose any other house and pour her expression of love into it just the same, reproducing a loving and well-organized home. So it is with the Kingdom of God. Heaven is a place where the Kingdom of God is expressed, and the Kingdom of God is made up of His virtues, which flow from His very being into whatever space He desires to fill. So His Kingdom is invisible to the naked eye, but when the Kingdom is expressed, its results are visible to all.

For this reason, the Kingdom of God can be reproduced in other places. Just as He created Heaven to be His headquarters, He decided to create another place to further His Kingdom. This place is called Earth. Here, the Kingdom is expressed through the hearts of those created in His image and likeness, the Kingdom man and the Kingdom woman. We allow His Kingdom to flow on Earth as it flows in Heaven.

Chapter 1

HER GRAND ENTRANCE

"And the Lord God said, 'It is not good that man should be alone. I will make him a helper comparable to him.'"
(New King James Version, Genesis 2:18)

Genesis 2 is a very important chapter for the Kingdom woman, and she should study it again and again. In that chapter, she was on the verge of making her grand entrance into the world. When God said that it was not good for man to be alone and that He would make him a helper comparable to him, it was not a mere thought that He uttered from His mind. Neither was it an implication about man's deficiency. Rather, it was a divine announcement. In a divine announcement, God makes a formal and open declaration and gives notification of His intentions. You must not take a divine announcement lightly. When He takes the time to announce something, you must stop what you are doing and give your complete attention to what He is saying in that moment. When He said that man should be made in "our" image and likeness, that was a statement of the difference between man and what He had already created. So His words should be held in the highest esteem.

In the Scriptures, we see that divine announcements were made when very important things were about to happen in the lives of certain individuals. Not only did these announcements affect the individuals' lives, but they also affected others' lives. Do you remember Zechariah? He received an announcement that his barren wife would bear a son by the name of John. It should be noted that these two were well into their years on earth. So naturally, having a child would be nothing short of a miracle. This announcement was so important that an angel named Gabriel was sent to Zechariah to help him understand the importance of the moment. The life of their son, John, would have a very important purpose. He would prepare for the coming Savior of the world.

Of course, we are all acquainted with the young virgin named Mary. Mary was visited by the same angel as Zechariah. He announced to her that she would conceive a son and that his name should be called Jesus and he would become the Savior of the world. When the angel first appeared, he assured Mary that she was highly favored and blessed among women. He did so to help her understand that he had come because she had found favor in the Lord's sight and that the miraculous

2

event that was about to take place would alter her life and the world forever.

Of course, we can't forget the occasion when God spoke to Jesus's companions from Heaven, saying that Jesus was His beloved Son and they should hear Him. Because God's Son was so important, He didn't leave the announcement to an angel or another man. He made it Himself. All these announcements were of great importance because they foretold that God would do something distinct on Earth. That's why we should not rush past the present announcement concerning the woman who is about to make her grand entrance into the world but meditate on it and allow it to speak to us. God Himself has decided to announce her coming.

Back to the Garden

After the Lord God declared that Adam shouldn't be alone, He gave Adam an assignment that entailed displaying his lordship by naming the living creatures that He had created. God was giving Adam a visual example of what He had just announced: As each of the living creatures had a feminine counterpart, man had to have one. As the living creatures were paraded before Adam, he noticed something very interesting. He noticed that he was alone but they came in twos—male and female. He realized the members of each pair had a similar appearance, the same purpose, and the ability to commune as one. That was why two were better than one. He had just received a revelation of what God had spoken.

Oftentimes, when we women hear the word "help," we automatically view ourselves as the lesser of two. We imagine ourselves being someone's maid or bringing them coffee. But that could not be further from the truth. We simply misunderstand what God means by "helper." The word "help" in the Hebrew language refers to God's kind of help. It's when God steps in and gives you what you need so that you can accomplish any goal, for He is Jehovah Ezer—this means "the Lord is our Help." So when woman entered the world, she stepped onto the scene as an "Ezer," which meant help sent from the Lord. She entered as the solution that would be needed to help man accomplish God's purpose on Earth.

This is not to indicate that man had a deficiency; he didn't. When man was made, he had unique characteristics. God equipped him for his purpose on Earth. But woman was the completion of what had been in God's mind from the beginning of the creation process. She was not a second thought. Bringing woman into the world had always been in the Master's plan. And we must look at the wisdom of God on the matter. He allowed man to be clearly seen, yet He revealed and escorted woman to give her as a gift.

THE PURPOSE OF THE KINGDOM WOMAN

*"Then the rib which the Lord God had taken from man
He made into a woman, and He brought her to the man.
And Adam said: "This is now bone of my bones and flesh of
my flesh; she shall be called Woman, because she was taken
out of Man." (New King James Version, Genesis 2:22–23)*

When God created woman, He took her straight from man. If
He'd wanted a completely different creature, He would have
gone back to the soil. Instead, He wanted someone that was
comparable to man. "Comparable" simply means "of equal
quality or likeness, made from the same flesh and the same
bones." She was meant to be of the same substance as the
man and yet different from him. So upon first meeting her,
man was amazed at what God had done, for the one would
now be two. He quickly recognized that she was like him
and a benefit to him and this was a good thing.

Her Original Purpose

It's funny how we miss things. We have in our possession
a book that tells us about the creation of everything and
its Creator. This Bible is filled with knowledge regarding
a period from the beginning of time until the end of time.
Yet we struggle to see what is right in front of us. Somehow,
we seem to separate the purpose of woman at creation from
that of man at creation. We see how he fit into the scheme of
things, yet we dismiss ourselves from what God pronounced
over man. When God was speaking to Adam, He was speaking

to the woman and all of mankind. Yes, she too was the object of His speech.

It's hard to know what God meant for us if we cannot understand His language when He speaks. He does not use language in the way we do. When we speak, we speak from our natural senses. We are led by what we like and what we don't like. We even use language idly. His speech is never idle because every time He speaks to something or someone, an infusion of purpose occurs. Thankfully, we can go back to God's original words and regain an understanding of our purpose.

> *"So, God created man in His own image, in the image of God created He him; male and female created He them. Then God blessed them, and God said unto them, 'Be fruitful and multiply; fill the earth, and subdue it; have dominion over the fish of the sea, over the birds of the air, and over every living thing that moves upon the earth.'"*
> *(New King James Version, Genesis 2:27–28)*

As we can plainly see in the Scriptures, man and woman have the same purpose to fulfill on Earth, yet they achieve this purpose from different positions. Both are needed to produce children. One of them alone cannot multiply and replenish the Earth. So when they were created, they were meant to cooperate.

The Fall – A New Normal

In Genesis 3, the Bible speaks about the sin of man and woman and its consequences. It is referred to as the Fall. If you read this chapter in its entirety, you will see man and woman transition from one condition to another. To fall is to be released from our former status to a lower status. The lower status is what we see in the world today. Along with this lower status came a loss of knowledge of who we originally were and how everything worked.

Man did not realize exactly what would result from disobeying God. The serpent did not grab the fruit, shove it in woman's mouth, and make her eat it. He gave her a very convincing story that caused her to make her own decision as to what she would do. She believed what he said and ate the fruit then convinced her husband to eat it, and he ate it. She did not force him to eat it either. After he ate the fruit, they began to see the consequences of their actions. Man and woman then realized that they had relinquished their earthly dominion.

Since the Fall, mankind has been trying to regain its original status. This is evident in the attempt to tame the animals that Adam previously named and had lordship over in the garden. It can also be seen in man's attempt to regain the airways through air travel, space travel, and the dispersing of satellites in the heavens. Since the ground was cursed, man has been striving to restore and preserve things found in nature. Man is still engaged in a struggle to master the waterways but has fallen short.

The Fall transformed the relationship between man and woman into a tussle over dominance and equality. They no longer knew how to honor and respect one another for their God-given differences. This can be seen in some countries and religions where men dominate women and force them into obedience. In other countries, women's rights movements are targeting equality in every area. Even in marriage unions, husbands and wives struggle to maintain the marriage covenant, usually ending up with high divorce rates. The marriage union was meant to never be broken. But when man and woman ate from the forbidden tree, they had no clue of the change that transpired. They lost what they had but gained a whole other knowledge base. Not only did they disobey God, but they also found out why He had given the command in the first place. To partake of the tree meant to experience what the tree offered, good and evil. So man and woman must now be rescued from the consequences of their disobedience.

As a woman, you are who you are. God made you as you are. If you learn to understand yourself and accept your makeup, you will gain better knowledge of your purpose as a woman and how to operate on Earth. You will also know how to give yourself what you need and how to relate to others. Many times, we fail ourselves by relinquishing our power and strength to others. In relationships, many women believe that it was the men who robbed them of something. The truth is, the women relinquished their own power. It's the story of Eve and the serpent.

Our Redemption Process

Redemption has to do with the process of regaining what was lost in exchange for payment. A lot of people think this means getting back personal items that were lost or taken. However, in this case, redemption refers to the process of regaining man's original status and regaining the possessions he received in the very beginning but subsequently lost. Since we could not do this ourselves, an intervention by God, the Father, was necessary. He sent His only begotten Son to pay the price required in order to retrieve what was lost.

It had to be His Son because as a matter of law, only our nearest kin could make the purchase and then reinstate us. This was the Kinsman-Redeemer. After all, there was no one else akin to man with the ability and status to purchase us back and reinstate us to our former positions.

God knew exactly what He was doing when He created us. He knew that sin would come into the world and that we would need to be redeemed. Part of our redemption process involves regaining the knowledge that the first man and woman had.

They knew their purpose on Earth. They knew their perspectives and their positions of operation, and they also knew what made the Kingdom flow properly. So our redemption process contains everything we need to know to properly reproduce God's Kingdom on Earth.

Chapter 2

HER PERSPECTIVE

When the fall of mankind occurred, one of the things that was lost was the woman's perspective. As Kingdom women, we were created to bring our unique perspective to the world. A perspective is the way one sees life, handles situations, solves problems, and relates to other people. Our perspective is different from that of the men God created. Our perspective is so unique that until we came on the scene, there was no one to express it. So unless we understand the importance of our God-given perspective and how it differs from men's and accept it, we will not fully appreciate our purpose.

As Kingdom women, we cannot misunderstand Genesis 2:18–24. If you believe that this is just a romantic love story between a man and his bride, your focus is off-center. Because this is one of the main Scriptures cited concerning marriage, we tend to overlook what it states about the woman and why she was placed on the earth. Many have gotten the idea that women were only created for marriage, making marriage their top priority. Thus, finding a mate becomes their purpose in their pursuit of happiness.

This causes the married woman to believe that she has obtained the prize and also creates a deficiency mindset where the single woman is concerned. It causes the married woman to believe that the single woman is not whole without a man. Moreover, it causes the single woman to believe she is not enough. Because she views herself as a rib without a body, she feels incomplete and alone. Adam and Eve were the first man and woman on Earth, so it was inevitable that they would marry in order to begin populating the earth. But that does not mean that every woman must get married to fulfill her divine purpose on the earth.

Because the creation story and the marriage story are so intertwined, we must train our minds to see that God created the woman to be complementary with the man. I say "with" because we tend to look at the man as the standard and the woman as an extra as if she was sent to merely give the man something to fill his time with. We also judge our importance based on who was created first. We believe that because the man was created first, he was more important. In doing so, we show that we do not understand God's creation process, and we make light of our purpose.

Consequences of the Fall of Man

When man and woman fell, they lost the ability to respect each other's perspective. Now, each of them views their opinion and perspective as being higher than the other's. The results of the fall of man and woman are evident in many ways. They include how we treat one another, how we compare ourselves to one another, and how we fear one another. Men tend to believe that they are stronger and wiser than women. Some believe that women don't have the ability to hold any high positions mainly because they believe that women are emotionally sensitive and vulnerable and cannot think straight. In the end, this causes disrespect and the inability to see women as their equals, comparable to them.

Likewise, the woman has a set of prejudices regarding the man. Many women believe that men are simple brutes. They believe that men are only good for what they can provide or what they can fix. Some believe that at heart, men are grown children who need a mother. A great number of women do not believe that men can be faithful in relationships. They expect men to be unfaithful, accusing them of being led by their sexual desires and not their God-given intelligence. All these things and more can be attributed to the fall of mankind. The scariest part of all this is that it has resulted in women not understanding the purpose and the importance of their perspective.

Intercourse

According to the Scriptures, God went into man and extracted a rib. Then God made woman out of man's rib. Man recognized that she came out of him because she was of the same flesh and bone as him. Then a statement was made as to this being the reason why a man would leave his father and mother. He would leave them to come together with his wife so that they would become one flesh again.

Returning to being one flesh requires intercourse. Only husbands and wives are given the right to indulge in sexual intercourse. But the concept of intercourse goes further than sex. Intercourse is the exchange of information and perspectives between two or more people. Man and woman were to become one by sharing their perspectives with one another. After all, just having sex did not constitute a full relationship. Man and woman would have to communicate to have a successful relationship.

Even though woman was taken from man and had the same likeness, she was his opposite. She did not exist in opposition to him but for him. We must understand that man was never meant to operate as a solitary man. That was why woman was created. From the solitary man came male and female as well as two perspectives: the masculine and the feminine. And merging the two minds took communication. After all, they were not opposite species; they just stood at opposite poles.

The feminine perspective gave the man the ability to have a system of checks and balances on the earth. Her perspective gave him a way to weigh things out. When she gave her opposing perspective, it caused him to expand his understanding and consider another viewpoint. This is not to say that her viewpoint was better than his. Rather, when the two perspectives came together, one big picture resulted. Our God sees one big picture, while we see a bunch of tiny little puzzle pieces that don't make sense. When He sees us operating together, He sees us as a whole. That's why our perspective as women is so important. If woman didn't lend man her lenses and he didn't lend her his, they would both be partly blind. Are you starting to see clearly now?

This is what I'm trying to convey to the single woman and to women at large. Even though the Bible refers to marriage as the example, you can look closer to see the purpose of the woman outside marriage. Marriage is so commonly used to display the unity of man and woman because it seems to be the easiest example to understand. The theme of marriage seems to appear frequently in the Scriptures to help people understand other concepts as well. When man and woman come together, the goal is not always marriage and certainly is not solely sexual intercourse.

Marriage is not the only context the woman needs to focus on here. Her focus should be the balance that was created when man and woman began to communicate. You don't have to be married to share the way you see things in the world. You don't need a husband to speak for you while you remain silent in the background. Your perspective speaks for itself. So whether you are single or married, you are a woman. It is your purpose to share a woman's perspective with the world. Yes, that includes what you think, how you feel about things, and how things affect you and other women in this world. A man's perspective alone can lead to all types of prejudices toward the woman. In essence, failure to hear the woman's perspective means that in many equations, her needs and desires will be put to the side. So, if the man does not decide to speak up for you, your voice will go unheard and imbalance will remain.

Earthly Counsel

"Plans are established by counsel; By wise counsel wage war."
(New King James Version, Proverbs 20:18)

When my husband watched movies, he usually liked the ones where the characters would explore unknown territories. In these movies, they would travel to places like deep space, the ocean deep, and the furthest points on the map, likely uninhabited by mankind. As I watched, I noticed that the groups of explorers had one thing in common: Each group gathered a team of people who were experts in their fields. Of course, they found the best captain they could to lead the team. And whenever there was a problem, the captain never just called the shots without first calling a meeting with his team of experts. When the team assembled, he asked questions, drawing from their expertise. He then took everything they said into consideration and made an informed decision. In other words, before he made any decisions, he needed to receive counsel in areas that he was not an expert in.

The purpose of a marriage between the two perspectives, masculine and feminine, was to produce perfect and complete counsel for use in governing the earth. The King James Bible Dictionary defines counsel as advice given upon deliberation or consultation. Hence, before a decision was made, the man and the woman would formally assemble, bringing both perspectives together and forming an earthly council. So man and woman would sit down, talk, listen to each other, and respect each other's perspective without feeling threatened.

In essence, you have just received a revelation of the word "help": someone of the same caliber as you to sit at the table and confer with; an expert in their God-given area to give you the understanding you need, which, coupled with your God-given expertise, will help you make an informed decision. This is ideal. After all, who makes an informed decision without examining all perspectives?

In the case of a husband and wife, many believe that the husband (man) has been given all understanding, all wisdom, and all knowledge. They also believe that he, the man, has no need to ask for anything outside of himself. So he could be ready to teach his wife everything as if she came to Earth with a blank slate for her mind. The reality is that when the woman was created, the Creator endowed her with special abilities that the husband (man) would need before he knew what he needed and before he could ask for help. So, the word "help" automatically gives the impression that the man cannot or should not do it alone. This means that the woman was equipped with what she would need to complete her portion of the task. So the man should always consider the woman to have whatever he doesn't have.

The Law of Inheritance

In the Scriptures, Numbers 27 presents an amazing example of how women used their perspective to change the laws of the land. According to the law at the time, if a man died, his inheritance went to his sons. If he had no sons, then the inheritance went to his brothers. As you can clearly see, there is no mention of the possibility of the man having any daughters. Can you imagine how the women in the land must have felt? Imagine how you'd feel if your father died and you received nothing in his will, yet he gave of his property and his money to others without concern regarding your well-being. This could cause any woman to feel like she was not important.

The story opens with the introduction of five women, the daughters of a man named Zelophehad who was deceased but had no sons. They would have been overlooked regarding inheritance from their father, and his property would have gone to his brothers. As a result, they would have faced the loss of their father's name to the clan.

These women believed that the law should be amended and that they should be given of their father's inheritance. So instead of moping around, they gathered together and approached their leader, the priest, and the entire congregation of leaders at the place where meetings occurred. They stated their claim, the claim was taken to God, and they received what they were asking for.

Knowing that they served a God who was just in His treatment gave them the confidence to allow their voices to be heard. So five women that were not spoken for by husbands or their father caused the laws of the land to be amended. Imagine that! They caused attention to be directed to an issue that, had they said nothing, would have continued to be handled in the same old way. However, because they spoke up, the women who came after them could reap the benefits.

Just imagine how the noise went abroad about these women, what joy and admiration other women must have felt. I'm sure that this began to awaken women's minds to the possibility of what could be accomplished for them. Now, think about

the women who came before them. I bet that they wished
that they had spoken up.

It is said that we, women, don't normally ask for what we
want. And if we do, we can't handle the criticism. These
women asked for what they wanted, and they got it. Now,
think of all the ideas that you've been holding inside. And
just imagine all the times you wanted to set the record straight
concerning what women could do.

Now, imagine what could have happened if you had
released the ideas. Imagine all the women that your words
could have impacted. Kingdom women, it's time for us to
open our mouths.

Conclusion

Kingdom woman, the ball is in your court. It is up to you to
understand your place in this world. No one is going to wait
for you to feel important enough to fulfil your God-given
purpose. Your perspective originated when God brought
you into the world. You alone are the lead voice on what it
is to be a woman. Do not allow any negative views of who
you are to become the way you view yourself. God, rather
than you or men, gave you your place.

You are everything that the Almighty has created you to be.
You have been created as one who deserves to be heard and
respected because you reflect the image of God. You don't

need the permission of those who will not listen. This is your place; it always was. If you have any doubts, remember that the Almighty God's work was not completed until after He introduced you to the world! Be released from your doubts, fears, and the feeling that you can't perform the task at hand. You were made for this. Kingdom women, open your mouths and release your perspective!

Chapter 3

HER AUTHORITY

Another area lost due to the fall of man was the recognition that women had authority on Earth. God has given the Kingdom woman authority on this earth. The purpose for giving her authority was to enable her to rule the earth along with the man. He established their authority before He placed them in the garden, before marriage was expressed, and even before establishing the church as we know it today. So, it was very important to Him that they knew what they were put on this earth to do.

While some women understand the authority that they have been given, many women struggle to understand their authority and how to function in it. Because of the fall of man, the systems of the world consider having authority to be synonymous with being a man. It's no wonder they have this mindset. From the beginning of time, we've seen outstanding evidence of men's contributions to this world.

So we've seen men's authority being exercised constantly, and though there are many examples of women with authority, because of their various personal experiences, it has been hard for some women to understand their authority and how to express it. They cannot comprehend it especially if they have never seen a clear picture up close or been given clear boundaries.

An added disadvantage is that some women don't believe women can be in positions of authority. So they go so far as to refer to other women as controlling or operating outside a woman's place. And yes, there are still women who think this way today. They believe that women outside the home or women who make more money than their husbands can't have successful marriages and are trying to wear the pants in their relationships. Thus, they contribute to oppressing other women. This must stop. It's bad enough when the opposite sex does it; having to also struggle against the minds of our sisters is disturbing. Being forced to fight someone who is supposed to be in the fight with you can sometimes weaken your stance and give the world the impression that you can't cooperate. This gives those who don't want us to take our place in this world evidence that supports their prejudices.

These women will also interfere with younger women by throwing confusing teachings into the mix. While some may not grasp their authority, others walk in fear. As they walk in fear, they do not operate in their authority because that would place them outside their comfort zone. They would fear losing what they had. Some women just want to be taken care of by a man, so seeing others operating in their authority can be quite intimidating to them. They consequently set themselves against those who are walking in their divine purpose. Then they become coconspirators with those that desire women to be oppressed.

Authority is a subject that Kingdom women should not ignore. Therefore, we must make a conscious effort to explore our God-given authority on Earth. It is not enough for us to have PhDs in submission and high school diplomas in the area of authority. As a matter of fact, they are so intertwined that one cannot be spoken of without the other. Together, they are like two sides of the same coin. So it is imperative that we, Kingdom women, refamiliarize ourselves with the subject in order to reform our understanding. Then we will be able to properly balance the two.

Authority is the power or right to make decisions and give orders that should be followed. So authority is a responsibility. This means that you can't just think about yourself; you must also think about others. Those in authority should be careful about how they treat the people who submit to them. And they must exercise proper judgment in making decisions. Authority should never be looked at as some form of celebrity. It is not a popularity contest. Anyone operating in any type of authority must be ready to serve by making sure everyone has what they need to do the job. So please remember that there is an authority higher than you: While you are someone's authority, you also submit to a higher authority.

The word "authority" brings both fear and pride to the hearts of men: fear because nobody wants another person to dominate them or take advantage of them, pride because many believe that they are more equipped or entitled to be the ones in authority. This is simply because they don't understand what authority is and how it is derived. Yet authority in the Kingdom of God was never meant to be a means of selfish expression. It was meant to be a further expression of God and how the Kingdom of God flowed.

Authority as a Position

In the Scriptures, we see varying levels of authority and that God gives all authority. Jesus is the only one that has received all authority in Heaven and on Earth. God has given the Kingdom woman her authority on Earth. She must know where her authority lies and where it does not. She cannot operate in the authority God has given her without first understanding the big picture, the Kingdom of God and what makes it flow. When we search the Scriptures, we see that the Kingdom of God is very orderly and operates with a system of titles and ranks, authority. We see the order of the Godhead, the Father, the Son, and the Holy Spirit. We see the order of the angels displayed in the Scriptures. We also see the order of governments and the order of the family. To be effective in her purpose, the Kingdom woman must find her position in the ranks. When she does that, she will find her position of authority. At that point, she can be set free to operate according to her divine capabilities.

At the age of 17, I joined the U.S. Army Reserves. The following summer, I was shipped off to basic training. It was a whole new world of discovery. Everyone was dressed alike, walked alike, and talked alike because they had their own culture. As soon as we got there, they gave us a booklet that included, among other things, the ranking system they used. It was our responsibility to learn the ranking system from the highest to the lowest levels. Thus, we could recognize who was who. This caused us to always know our place/position, that is, who had authority over us and whom we had authority over.

Not only did we learn to recognize rank, but we also had to recognize positions. A position is simply where someone or something is put or located. Your ranking was not necessarily a direct job assignment. Although you carried status, you had to be placed in a said position in order to operate in your authority. We were given job assignments and placed in positions to operate. Then we were able to express our levels of authority. Without proper placement, we had no one to command directly and no job assignments. Those with higher status levels received the respect of recognition in their presence.

Authority can never be generic. It must be derived from somewhere or someone. No one except God's Son has authority over everything and everybody. So, everyone is either submitting to an authority or has someone submitting to their authority. There is no authority assumed out of nowhere that no one except the authority figure knows about. You must operate within an already established order. That's why genuine authority wants you to know who and what you are submitting to. Everyone knows exactly what their assignment is and who is in their chain of command. Fake authority does not want to operate with clarity. So it likes to blur the boundary lines so that you do not know where its authority begins or ends. People who do this leave room for themselves to manipulate others.

Authority is not ownership. Someone else has given you your position of authority. That means you could also be removed from said authority. Your authority is limited to your assignment. So your authority has boundaries, and there are limitations on how much power you can have over a person. That person does not become your personal slave. Even though God has given you authority, you must operate in it by faith. You must trust that those you have authority over, even men, will receive you. You should step out in faith and allow God to give you wisdom in the matter. At no time are you to operate by intimidating, dominating, or manipulating. Operating in that way would be against the God-ordained order.

Authority has absolutely nothing to do with gender. Otherwise, women would have no rightful authority over their children or would be unable to teach in classrooms because they would not be able to demand obedience from their students. Authority has everything to do with your position and what you have been given. You cannot think that just because you are female, you have less authority. You must let go of the notion that the voice of a woman carries less weight in the world. Many women since the beginning of time have been noted for the changes that have resulted from their using their voices. Not every woman was in a leadership position. But that does not mean that they were not influential at all. Just as those that were held in slavery had to declare their way to freedom, the Kingdom woman must use her authority and influence in whatever position she finds herself in. So know that whatever position you find yourself in, you have the power to shift your circumstances directly or indirectly.

Her Authority in Marriage

We must be careful in our approach to this subject. It is vital that we handle the associated conversation with the wisdom of God simply because this is an area that the fall of man has hit hard. When you speak of the authority of the wife to some who are deeply religious, you must get ready for a fight. Many men do not want to identify their wives as having authority except over the children or regarding going to the grocery store. Some are not interested in having to listen to a woman talk let alone share her thoughts on how things could be done. Nor do some men want to consider their wives as equals. Yet it is imperative that we have this conversation. We can no longer consider single women to be free and married women to have surrendered to bondage. Marriage was never meant to be a place of bondage but one of agreement. The man and woman were meant to understand their positions in the marriage to produce a smooth flow in the home.

It is very interesting that when a woman is married or considering marriage, the subject of submission is usually the only thing that's taught. Of course, submission is *super* important when teaching on marriage! However, her authority as a wife should also be discussed in those teaching sessions. Submission teaches one to flow with the leader, that is, how to receive and obey instructions. In comparison, authority teaches one to flow as a leader, that is, how to make decisions and give instructions. We should be careful to depict the wife as one who is under authority yet in authority.

I believe that this will change how the wife is viewed and how she views herself simply because it will cause her mind to shift to her expectations in the marriage and—oh, yeah—her husband's expectations of her. So, if wives believe that they can share in the responsibility of leading, their posture will change, and they will keep their thinking caps on. This will also bring respect and honor to their position.

Nowhere am I saying that the wife has authority over her husband. What I am saying is that since authority comes at different levels and with different parameters, in marriage, the wife occupies the next level of authority. This is parallel to what the vice president is to the president: If the president is taken captive or dies, she has to assume the position of the leader. If he goes on a long journey, it doesn't matter; she has to assume full responsibility.

Being the closest person to the leadership position, she should be knowledgeable about everything that's happening and equipped to make decisions. So it is with the wife. She should be viewed as a leader who needs to be knowledgeable about everything that's going on in their relationship and household business. In the event of things like her husband being taken captive by sickness or abandoning his post through divorce or death, even though she is grieving, she should be capable of taking the helm.

If you were to ask most people the question, "What kind of authority does a wife have?" the answer would be, "She has authority over the children." Yes, this is true. However, she can express her authority in a much broader way. So she should anticipate uncovered areas where her family is concerned and be ready to step into position. Even while married and submitting to her husband, she can operate in a position of authority in the world. This is the case simply because authority is a position, and no matter what position the woman is in, she will always bring with her the unique genius that God put inside her.

I am a firm believer that whatever you teach your children should come not only from what you say but also from what you display. How can they follow a pattern if the pattern is not displayed on a continual basis during various situations in the relationship? It is often said that children do what you do and not what you say. So we should let them see a working model. And this way, they can learn through repetition, and the lessons will be engraved in their minds. Both the husband and the wife should remember that they are enacting their knowledge of God-ordained roles in the marriage.

Another area of the wife's authority is apparent when she prays. I believe that if you don't understand your purpose as a wife and believer, your prayers can be hindered. We, women and, of course, wives pray for things that God has already given us. If we have knowledge of who we are and what's ours, then our prayers should sound different. If the things in our lives don't align with what we know should happen, we should use our God-given authority in prayer to break down and move everything that would interfere with the way things should be. Then we should use our authority in prayer to do what our Heavenly Father did just before He created us—he made an open announcement establishing the right way. Know this: Both the courts of Heaven and the gates of hell recognize who we are and our authority in the home, and so should we.

Men and women must all understand that we are here to help cover the man. We were not placed here for ourselves and to get what we wanted while leaving the man uncovered. We were placed here to cover one another naturally and spiritually. So it is possible that women who married without knowing their God-given authority are not covering their husbands because they assume that since the men are the heads of the unions, it is their job to cover the women and the women's job to cover the kids but not the men. The woman should be able to communicate to her husband what information she needs to do her job. If he is not cooperating, once again, she should use her authority in prayer to establish God-ordained order in the home.

Make no mistake about it: This understanding should also be expressed regarding the single woman. However, it really doesn't matter if you are married or single. What matters is that you are a woman. A man may not be your husband, but so what? God has given you the authority to cover him with the knowledge you have from your perspective on matters and prayer. Whether world affairs, business, child-rearing, health, or anything else is concerned, the man needs us to be there, walking in our dominion. Remember, God did not give the man everything, He gave the woman what He wanted her to have to balance things out. So, whether you are married or not, now that you have the right information, grab a seat at the table and exercise your authority regardless of the situation you find yourself in!

You would have to be both deaf and blind not see the woman operating in her authority today. And you would have to be in utter denial given that a woman holds the role of vice president. Women all over the world are recognizing who they are and what they have the authority to do, so get ready to see more. I believe that many women are on the verge of stepping onto the scene. After all, they are being recognized and trained like never before. And when they show up, they will do so believing that they must be twice as prepared as men to prove themselves.

Chapter 4

HER SUBMISSION

The Kingdom woman is a submissive woman. The area of submission can be very tricky to the ears and the hearts of individuals. If we look at it through the narrow-mindedness of self, then we will not understand what submission really means. We believe submission has to do with being last, being soft-spoken, and holding our heads down while someone else tramples on us at their own pleasure. For this reason, many men and women are refusing to get married and to operate in their God-given roles in creation, and many are fatherless in the body of Christ. The fatherless ones are those who reject direction, correction, and an arc of protection. In other words, they refuse to submit to a set atmosphere or individual who has the spirit of the Father. Because they refuse to submit, they move around like wanderers, trying to find a place of rest.

Submission is a role that must be confronted if we are to operate according to the standards of the Kingdom. We cannot be afraid to address it. Because so many are afraid to dive into this subject, it is uncomfortable to talk about. We must humble ourselves and be ready to display God's purest image of submission on the earth. Many are afraid of submission. So unless it is properly addressed, many will resist it at all costs.

We cannot have authority on the earth without having submission on the earth. Both are needed and should work in synchrony. Because authority gives an individual the right to give instructions to others, there must be someone ready to receive and perform those instructions. Submission is an expression of God that gives another person the right-of-way to operate within her God-given role and its parameters. So there must be someone operating in authority before submission can occur.

Perfect submission is evident when you give it of your own free will. When we understand that we are submitting to God and the laws of His Kingdom, we can also submit to a person who is operating in their God-given authority. Submission was not designed to be taken from you. Neither should it be given through obligation or fear. This would indicate some type of control by the other person involved. When some sort of verbal threat or physical harm is implied, then there is abuse. But when submission is executed properly, there is a smooth flow of operation throughout the Kingdom of God.

Submission is not slavery. Slavery is the condition of owning a person without regard for their life's purpose. It bypasses another person's will and desire for personal satisfaction. It overlooks another person's strengths and weaknesses. It exploits a person's abilities for personal gain and gives the person little or nothing in return. We were not called to give ourselves as slaves to others. To do so would allow those in authority to walk all over us while we served them with no expectation of the will of God being enforced to address their disobedience. This is called abuse of authority. Your submitting to another serves a godly purpose. And that purpose does not concern fulfilling ignorant and fleshly whims. So submission has parameters.

Submission Is a Power

As Kingdom women, we must understand that our submission is our responsibility. It has been given to us to govern when and to whom to submit as directed by God. We can choose to submit to someone or cease to submit at any point in time. This is called free will. Free will gives you the ability to make good or bad decisions. It gives you the ability to think for yourself and consider the possible outcomes of the choices that will be made.

Our submission is a superpower. It is like the secret weapon of a warrior, given to us as we are disguised as an innocent sheep. A sheep's noteworthy characteristic is that it is non-threatening. When you think of a sheep, you think of someone who is led and does not think for herself. A sheep is considered dumb. It is considered to only be able to receive commands and carry them out. So "sheep" is thought to be an insult, but only by those that are arrogant. The reality is that if you give people instructions and they can do what's required, they sound quite intelligent.

When we use our submission correctly, we help those in authority to carry out plans that they themselves cannot handle alone. We become the arms and legs that reach and expand the mission of God. Without submission, the mission of God would be stunted. There would be no one to help execute His plans.

We cannot afford to give something so precious to the wrong person. If we give our submission to the wrong person, then we give that person something that they are not entitled to. We give our power over to someone who does not care about God's purpose on Earth. So your submission is something of value, and you must use your power to choose whom to give your service to. Because you should give submission of your own free will, if you choose not to submit to the rightful authority, you will reap the consequences of your decision.

Submission and Marriage

Submission in marriage can be a weighty topic as well. One reason for this is that marriage comes with its own set order that cannot be violated. Some men and women have the wrong view of the definition and parameters of submission. Some men view submission as confirming their God-given right to control their wives. And this is where the fear comes in for women. They fear that being married means being controlled by the man and that his desires will be the only ones fulfilled.

So the idea of marriage becomes offensive to women. And this is one reason why women are not highly enthused about marriage. These men and women forget our original purpose from the time of creation. They forget that man's being the head of the marital union under Christ is the divine order. According to His design, this system should produce a smooth way to transfer instructions from one person to another. It was never meant to suppress the woman. It was a means for the man and woman to submit to God's mission for *both* of them.

In the early years of my marriage, the women in the church taught me about my responsibility in marriage. They taught me that my responsibility was at home. They also taught me of my responsibility to the children that we would have. Then they told me how I was to serve my husband by cooking, cleaning, and making sure the children were clean and groomed when he arrived. I slowly began to feel resentment towards these ladies. You may wonder why. Maybe you already know why. These women continuously told me what my responsibilities and duties were without explaining what his responsibilities and duties were. I felt that they were laying burden after burden upon me while he had no responsibility to me, the house, and the children. Only I was to submit to him without any expectation of receiving any return on my investment.

You see, they explained marriage and submission to me in the form of performance and duties. I could only see myself with a child in one hand and a clothes basket in another. They stripped away the blessings of being a wife and made me want to reconsider it. I began to give my husband the side-eye and to think, like many other women did, that marriage was a way to take away my freedom.

Thank God for the Scriptures because they encouraged me to understand marriage as a more balanced relationship model. The Scriptures gave me the ability to see both my husband's responsibility as a husband as well as mine as a wife. It laid out the duties of a husband in plain English. It explained how he was to treat me and the children. It set the parameters for what he could do, what he could not do, and what would hinder his prayers. The Scriptures spoke of me with such care and consideration that I blushed! They truly began to change my expectations regarding marriage, and my fear of submitting to him diminished.

Submission is not gender-associated. It is not limited to the woman, and neither is it limited to the confines of marriage. As a matter of fact, marriage is the only place where a woman is told directly to submit to a man. She is not to submit to men in general as this would be utter chaos, implying that the woman was less than the man. But she is to submit to her husband. The command to submit is given to all to profit everyone. It is an extension of the flow of Kingdom order. That's why we must know when and where we should submit. Being a submissive wife to someone other than your husband is out of order.

In the context of marriage, the woman is to submit to God by submitting to her husband. In addition, the husband is to submit to God by loving his wife like Christ loved the church and laid down his life for her. It is the man's responsibility to submit to what God has placed inside his wife, for those who misjudge submission in marriage misjudge the loving relationship of God and His people. A husband that submits to God and lays down his life for his wife epitomizes selflessness. This is the type of relationship that one should run to, not from.

Remember, woman was made for man, but man himself did not make her. Neither did woman create him. God is the one that created both. He is also the Creator of marriage. He alone defines the parameters of what it shall be. I say this to help you understand that when we get married, we start on a path of discovering one another. That means that we allow God's full purpose of marriage to unfold in our relationship. This understanding should never put you at odds with your spouse; rather, it should give you the right perspective as you learn to operate as a spouse.

It is a fact that if you don't know how to use something, you will break it. That's why instructions accompany every product you buy. Many of us never read the instructions and then rely on our own intelligence. Then, when we break the thing, we then turn to the instructions. We have been given instructions for marriage in the Scriptures, yet we don't follow them. We must understand what God is after in marriage. He is a God who has made us in His image. So He is interested in seeing His reflection on the earth. When the marriage of authority and submission is on proper display, the two people learn to operate not merely as themselves, but as one person.

The Marriage of Authority and Submission

You must understand that Adam and Eve knew about walking in authority as well as walking in submission. A lot of people look at them as being innocent people who were new to this world. But the two knew things that we are now discovering. When they arrived on the earth, they were fully equipped to rule. They were already given their directives. And they knew that the earth as well as its inhabitants were to submit to them. They intrinsically knew how to operate in unison, well, at least until the day of the serpent's temptation of the first woman.

At that point, no animal had ever attacked man or woman. No bug had ever bitten or stung them. There was no sin on the earth, so there was no killing, and the animals did not attempt to rule over them. The recognition of authority by way of submission was in their DNA. There was also no implication that God had given man and woman a desk along with pen and paper to take notes, for their Creator alone was their mentor. And there was no need for paper because what mattered was written on the tablets of their hearts. They were allowing the Kingdom of God to flow through them.

Submission Is a Position

Submission is also a position that we operate from. Sometimes, we are so worried about whose position has the most control or which position people admire the most. It's usually the most visible position. The crazy part is that we, Kingdom women, can be in positions of submission in one area of life but in positions of authority in another area. That's why it is important that you understand submission as a position and not as being less than another person. You must learn to detach as much ego as possible from it. If you don't, you will not be able to glide from submission to authority without carrying baggage with you. And if you think being in a position of submission is a weakness, then what do you think of married women, children, and those you may employ? Believe me, your thoughts about others will show up in one way or another.

Once, when I was perusing over the different branches of the military, I noticed that they had different areas of expertise, yet they assisted each other in fighting the same wars. The U.S. Airforce mainly focuses on the air and the U.S. Army on the land. The U.S. Marines assist in various ways, and the U.S. Navy mainly operates in the seas. These branches of the military may not operate from the same positions, but all those areas need to be covered.

Now, the branch that operates in submarines under the sea should not become envious of the branch that flies high above the waters. So the branch that fights from underneath cannot afford to become so offended with its positioning that it walks off post, leaving its position unmanned. If it were to do that, the enemy would have access to an entrance, and that could be devastating to our country. If the enemy ever succeeded in penetrating our borders, untrained civilians would have to fend for themselves.

In basic training, we could never leave our positions before our replacements came to relieve us of our duties. If they failed to show up on time, we remained in those positions until others were assigned to them. If one just up and deserted her position, she would leave the next person with no one to cover their back. So you can imagine the implications of being in a battle alone. That was why we were never meant to be in a situation alone. Alone, we could have been overtaken easily. So we must humble ourselves and understand that submission is a very important position that makes the Kingdom of God flow smoothly.

Chapter 5

HER LEGACY

The Kingdom woman knows she must leave her legacy to the next generation of Kingdom women. This legacy is composed of the wisdom, knowledge, and understanding she has gained over the course of the various seasons of her life. She cannot leave the next generation of Kingdom women to fend for themselves without proper guidance because each generation does not have years and years of trial and error to acquire the knowledge she already possesses. Just as the earthly, sensual woman is out to spread her ungodly knowledge, the Kingdom woman must be ready and available to share what she has. She cannot allow the sensual woman to be at the forefront, imparting her ungodly ways to the next generation of women.

The sensual woman is tremendously different from the godly woman. Instead of pleasing God, she seeks to gratify herself. She is only after what pleases her five senses. Imagine this woman sharing her ideas about how to get a man or husband. Imagine the extent to which she uses games and manipulations to get what she wants. Our young women and young girls would be fed nonsense that would cause them to give themselves to men at a price. If you don't leave instructions, other women just like you will be left at the mercy of the sensual woman: *"So in Christ we, though many, form one body, and each member belongs to all the others"* *(New International Version, Romans 12:5).*

For the Kingdom woman to leave a legacy, she must understand that every victory won and all ground gained does not belong to her alone. She is a member of a network of believers who share information and should be like-minded. She cannot wait until she's on her deathbed to share with other Kingdom women. She must get her wisdom out as soon as she obtains it and pass it on. In this way, the legacy will be in operation before her passing, and nothing will be lost.

Passing knowledge along as you go is like running a relay race. No one runs a relay race by themselves. It must be run as a team. This way, each member of the team has a part to play. No one can win or lose without the others. Each team member must successfully pass the baton to another for the team to win. If anyone does not pass the baton correctly, then the whole team loses. By taking the baton, a person becomes responsible for passing it to the next teammate. Similarly, when we pass on what we've learned, the next person takes on the responsibility of continuing the legacy.

The Kingdom woman must not be deceived into believing that since we all have the same Bible, we have the same information. We do not. Since we interpret things from our own worldviews, we only understand things from the perspectives of our environments and our upbringings. Not every home was a model home (by "model home," I mean perfect in every way). Adam and Eve were in the most perfect environment anyone could ask for. But before long, they made mistakes too. Maybe they needed role models.

Many did not have fathers in the home, and those that did had often had physically, emotionally, or spiritually absent fathers. Moreover, their mothers had to work and to carry the load themselves and were not able to be fully present. In some homes, others had to step in to help. Many were raised by uncles, aunts, and grandparents. Some were even raised by older brothers or sisters. So women's backgrounds vary in terms of what they received from their upbringings.

The woman's environment outside the home also played a role in her development. Many women have been influenced by women in their communities. Among the latter are neighbors, teachers, and the women at church who decided to take them under their wings. Let's not forget about the internet. The internet is responsible for a lot of what we see today. Sometimes the influences are bad. When a child is left to herself, she becomes prey that gangs and other bad groups can scoop up. Ultimately, she will form her own conclusions about life. This is the reason we must pass on what we know: Without us, she would be lost.

Transparency

When sharing her legacy with other women, the Kingdom woman must be as transparent as possible. Transparency is not the condition of unveiling all the details in your life. It is not necessary to share certain things with others. It does not help them to grow. If you share too much of the wrong information, the woman you are speaking to may not be able to handle it. Then you run the risk of scaring her away. Once she loses respect for you, all hope of pouring into her life is gone.

Transparency is the condition of being upfront and clear concerning who you are and what you've come to do. With transparency, there are no hidden agendas or motives. The person's intent is clearly seen and expressed in what they say and do. So when sharing with someone else, it is very important to remember that you are working for the Lord. Otherwise, you will believe that whatever she does, right or wrong, is a direct reflection of you. You must understand, however, that no one is perfect, and she must have the opportunity to make mistakes along the way.

The Kingdom woman must be wise in her sharing. Not every woman is ready to receive the understanding that she has. Some cannot handle the weight of her words or the soundness of her wisdom. She must be discerning regarding the levels of the women she imparts knowledge to. Some women are younger in their faith and require foundational teachings. There are also older women who haven't had the opportunity to be privy to this wisdom. They, too, will need parts of their foundations to be restructured. This will cause the Kingdom woman to spend some time dealing with their pasts in order to move forward. Whatever the case, she must be ready to deal with them at the levels they are at in their lives.

The Kingdom woman must understand that her mistakes are a good source of learning as well. Because of her mistakes, she now knows why right is right and wrong is wrong. She understands how the desires of her heart drew her out. Moreover, she is familiar with the tactics that were used against her. When one is on the right path, she does not get to experience some bad things personally. But when she is on the wrong path, she ends up in places she never thought possible. Many women have gone through unnecessary hardships and have found it hard to get back on course. But with the grace of God, all things are possible to the Kingdom woman if she believes.

This information is valuable for knowing what happens when one veers off the path and how to get back on course.

So the Kingdom woman should also view her mistakes and recovery as part of her arsenal against the enemy. She should never be ashamed, especially since she has overcome. She cannot use this as a reason to veer off course. Some believe that the dirtier one gets, the better. This is a myth and a waste of time because one may never get back on course. The information of the woman who never made it back is limited as she cannot lead others where she has never been.

The Kingdom woman must have her mission in mind from the beginning. She cannot allow herself to be so emotionally engulfed in the individual she is guiding that she loses sight of her agenda. She must view herself as the one who has come with solutions that will free the individual from her present state of being. She must also understand that her mission may pertain to a season. Not all relationships are meant to last a lifetime. In such cases, she must be comfortable releasing her mentee to the next level of growth and moving forward with her next mission.

Knowing Whom to Teach

The Kingdom woman must be able to recognize whom she can teach and whom she cannot teach. The woman that she encounters must have certain characteristics. She must be teachable and willing to learn. She must be ready to make the changes necessary. She must also be willing to prioritize her time, showing that she values the wisdom that she receives. If she refuses to carve out time, then she is refusing to honor the Kingdom woman and her time. If there are no extreme circumstances surrounding her, then she should be able to establish some type of time management. Watching a television series or going to the mall with friends is not a priority. So this relationship should not be the last thing on her agenda. Change starts somewhere; why not here?

The Kingdom woman must also choose a woman that is open and honest. If her mentee refuses to tell the truth, this will become an obstacle to helping her. No one wants to beg a person to let her help her. So her communication must be honest and clear. This woman should understand that she must voluntarily submit herself to the process. No one should have to make her do anything. She must also understand that even though her mentor has come to help, the mentor is not there to carry all her burdens on her shoulders. She is there to show her how to lighten the load. It's okay to become friendly, but respect must be maintained. When respect is no longer present, the purpose for being there has come to an end.

When helping another woman, you must be careful to ensure that she is listening and obeying instructions. If she is not following any of the directions you give her, then you must call her on the carpet. You should not be mean but direct. You are not there to just keep her company. Don't allow her to make you do all the work. If she is to benefit from the relationship, then she must put in time and effort. If you reach a place of anger and frustration, change strategies. Make her come to you and ask questions instead of chasing her down. Remember, your time and your wisdom are costly. Do not allow another to esteem them lightly. What you are giving her for free others are willing to pay for.

Sharing the Legacy

Imagine yourself at the age of 99. Imagine all the wisdom you've gained over the years. Think about all of the life situations you have faced and overcome. Call to remembrance the things that scared your socks off. Estimate the number of books you've read, and think about how much of the Bible you had the opportunity to familiarize yourself with. Even think of the things that others showed you over the years. Consider the things that you've witnessed due to those around you. Whew! What a vast amount of information you have inside you. You have so much wisdom to share with the generations that follow you.

The legacy of the Kingdom woman is so important that it must be shared with as many women as possible. We cannot afford to house all this information inside a coffin. We have a responsibility to other women that are up and coming in the body of Christ. We must realize that many are trying to make their own way. Many have hit roadblocks and don't know what to do. They need us to answer the questions that are circulating in their minds. Some don't even know they need help, but they need it, and this is where we come in.

One-on-One

One way to share your legacy is to avail yourself for one-on-one interactions. You can do this type of sharing in person, over the phone, or online. There are those who need someone to make personal time for them because they didn't have this type of guidance in their personal lives. They will need someone close to them who will fill that need. If you are up close, your mentee woman will have the ability to observe what you do as well as what you say. We all know that what we see impacts what we can do, so let's not shy away from up-close interactions with up-and-coming Kingdom women.

Group Mentoring

Not all sharing will be done one-on-one. Group mentoring is sharing with a small or larger group. This is an opportunity to share with more than one woman at a time. It will also give you room to have a hand in spreading your legacy faster. Many mentoring groups meet in person or online. Group mentoring could take the form of classes, seminars, and conferences. This would be a blessing to women of all ages. Remember, not everyone had the opportunity to learn in their environments, so they are constantly looking for opportunities to get connected to women who will share with them what they do not know. Also remember, what one woman does not want for free other woman will pay for.

Writing

Another way you can share the legacy is through writing. The purpose of writing is to share what you know with all who will read it. It gives you the ability to touch people from far off. Many people's lives have changed just because they opened the pages of a book or read other writing like blogs. The writer gives the reader the ability to tap into their insight. Many people write books and other manuscripts about topics like witchcraft, stealing cars, and the benefits of being a side chick. So why not write about the things that you have learned over the years? Besides, even the Bible was put into print so that everyone could study it at will.

Video/Audio

Video and audio are excellent ways to share your legacy. Your messages could be passed on from one generation to another. This would give the people watching/listening the ability to access them any time they needed to. Think about it: If we were not there when messages were shared, we would have the chance to watch/listen to them until we got them. Some people think that this is impersonal, but the availability of such a resource could be devastating to the Kingdom of Darkness.

This is exactly what we are trying to accomplish. Every woman must be able to access what she needs not just for her sake but also for those who come after her. Besides, if the world is using all these features and more, why can't we use them?

CONCLUSION

Get off the Bench!

Kingdom women, we must not view ourselves with passivity of mind. God placed us here on Earth to serve the purpose that He gave us. However, we must be settled in our minds regarding what that purpose is. We must also agree that we will not watch life from the bleachers or sit on the sidelines cheering on our men and that we refuse to let others' thoughts and intents bench us.

A lot of women believe that in every situation, they must be the supporters, nurturers, and cheerleaders. They run behind others and cheer them on. They get up behind them and push them forward while remaining in the background. Sure, their families adore them for it. Their friends adore them for it too. But when they don't concentrate on themselves, they don't give others a chance to cheer them on. As a result, those others believe that it's these women's job to stay back and cheer them on while they remain just fine in the background.

If you are one of those women, it's now time for others to back you up. Although your role comes naturally to you, you must begin to take a step forward and allow others to follow you. It may take some adjustment, but believe me, it is not the end of your cheerleading days. I mean, look at the word "cheerleader" again, and let me tell you what I see. I see "cheering as a leader." What's happened is that you've switched from pushing them forward and cheering them from the background to cheering for them as you lead them forward from the front. How amazing is this? You still get to be the supporter, nurturer, and cheerleader.

I would like men to know something: God made you in His own image and likeness. God has specific work for you to do. So we, women, are not here to take from you or to demote you from your God-ordained position. But you must understand that we, women, being made in God's image and likeness too, have been promised a place in this world. So we have come to take our God-ordained position. If any of us seem angry, then you must understand that we are fighting against others' mindsets. We are also fighting against traditions that won't die. We are at war with ourselves as well as the world.

So some degree of pushback is necessary for us to achieve what we were sent to do. But please don't misunderstand. We have no intent to fight against them as men. Oh, and please do understand that some degree of warfare is necessary to achieve this goal. We are asking you to help make way for us and to prepare to sit with more of us at the table.

As Kingdom women, we must educate ourselves to deal with the possible adverse attitudes of men in this world. By being aware of these attitudes, we know what we will encounter and can prepare ourselves to finesse our way through. Possible attitudes are anger, rejection, retaliation, sabotage, displays of pettiness, criticism, envy, intimidation, and fear of loss due to more qualified candidates' arrival at the table.

Women, let us put aside all thoughts of men as the enemies of our progress, and let us operate in a way that divinely says that we are promoting a complete image of God on Earth, not competition. Women, how we treat men is very important. We must understand that the same adversary that has us viewing men as our enemies has them thinking that we are their enemies. So, as we come into this new understanding, we must realize that men, too, have some growing to do. We must train ourselves not to treat men as our enemies but to view them as our fellow citizens on the earth. When we do this, we will allow the Kingdom of God to flow as it should! That is when men and women will bring their respect of one another to the table to rule together.

The reality is that we must pray for our men. This is because some things are locked up inside us, and when they come out in full force, those of our men who have not been enthusiastic about their wives and other women in powerful positions may feel uncomfortable. This may cause a disruption in the home, and where there is disagreement in the home, the enemy will be sure to make it his playground.

Remember, the Almighty created you for this. Also remember, you were sent to help the man. Don't take the word "help" to mean it's all about him. It is important that we start from the beginning and work our way backward through the story so that we remember what really happened. Remember, the Almighty started with one, and then the one became two. This was not a statement of man's superiority and woman's inferiority. It was just the Creator walking us through His thought process concerning His creation.

Before I conclude this portion, we must address something. Many of us women believe that in order to fulfill our purpose and be successful, we must walk away from our spouses. Many believe they can't have both. Not only do they leave their spouses, but they also believe that they must leave their children. Kingdom women, we've seen this behavior before. Sometimes men feel they need to leave their wives and children while reaching for success. Then, after succeeding, they want to regain their relationships with their children, hoping to repair the years of hurt and abandonment. Some may not be able to rekindle relationships with their wives, so they simply move on to other mates.

Some of you have personally felt victimized by such behavior. So let's not leave a legacy of broken relationships behind us if we can help it. It is possible to have family and purpose-linked success. You must understand that marriage and the family are just as much a part of your purpose as what you do outside the home. So it is possible to keep the family together and take your place in this world. When God gave the man a wife, He did not change His mind about their dominating the earth. Our marriages are very much a part of His plan for us. Since the Creator didn't think that the man should be alone, He must have felt the same way about the woman.

So listen, women, you can no longer despise men for taking your place. Before now, some of you never knew you could have a seat at the table. You can no longer despise other women for stepping up and standing in the places you were afraid to stand in. So don't just dream about achieving, do something about it. And don't be afraid to bring your femininity with you. Bring your pink laptops, your pretty dresses, your rose-petal scent, and your dangling earrings, and don't be afraid to be a woman in those environments.

Women, you were given to men as a gift, companions in matters of the earth. Be restored in your thinking, be restored in your desire to rule, not over men but with men. And remember to be ladies and open doors for the women that are up and coming. Do sift out those women who have slipped through but should not be there. Not all women are ready to be in those positions, but in their own time, they will be ready. So be careful not to fight over how many seats there are at the table; there are many tables, not just one. Operate in your purpose, and don't forget how the Kingdom of God flows.

Finally, Kingdom women, I am convinced in my mind that we should have the same understanding about our purpose. That way, we will be able to stay in our lanes. When we don't understand who we are and know how to operate in the Kingdom of God, we step over into other women's lanes. So it is my prayer that all you have read will change your heart regarding yourself and others.

I pray that you now have the courage to walk in your authority, your submission, and your perspective and to leave a legacy for the next generation of Kingdom women. For this is the purpose of the Kingdom woman, and this is how the Kingdom of God flows.

KINGDOM WOMEN DON'TS

✠ Single women, do not despise married women who submit to their husbands. Their husbands are their gifts from God.

✠ Married women, do not despise single women for being individuals. Being an individual is a gift of God.

✠ Older women, do not despise younger women, for you were once young.

✠ Younger women, do not despise older women, for soon you will be old.

✠ Kingdom women, do not disrespect other women because, when you do, you disrespect the image of God.

✠ Kingdom women working outside the home, do not despise women working in the home because you are all special in the eyes of God.

✠ Kingdom women working in the home, do not despise women working outside the home because you have a place there too.

✠ Kingdom women, do not despise men because God has determined their roles in the Kingdom as he has yours.

✠ Kingdom women, do not imitate masculine expression because feminine expression is much needed on the earth.

✠ Kingdom women, do not fight over a seat at the table, for there are many tables and you could create other tables.

✠ Kingdom women, do not fear to be who you are because you are a gift to the world.

How to Enter the Kingdom of God

If you have not taken the steps to become a Kingdom woman, this is what you need to do:

"That if you confess with your mouth the Lord Jesus and believe in your heart that God raised Him from the dead, you will be saved. For with the heart one believes unto righteousness, and with the mouth, confession is made unto salvation" (New King James Version, Romans 10:9–10).

Let us pray! Father God, I ask You to forgive me my sins. I believe in my heart and confess with my mouth that Your Son, Jesus, died on the cross for my sins and that You raised Him from the dead. Lord Jesus, I ask you into my heart as my Lord, Savior, and King. Teach me how to be the Kingdom woman that you have created me to be and how to let the Kingdom of God flow through my heart!

Thank you.

Amen!

www.ingramcontent.com/pod-product-compliance
Lightning Source LLC
LaVergne TN
LVHW021618080426
835510LV00019B/2640